SIMON SPOTLIGHT
An imprint of Simon & Schuster Children's Publishing Division
1230 Avenue of the Americas, New York, New York 10020
This Simon Spotlight edition January 2020
Text copyright © 2020 by Marilyn Singer
Illustrations copyright © 2020 by Lucy Semple
For information about special discounts for bulk purchases, please contact
Simon & Schuster Special Sales at 1-866-506-1949 or business@simonandschuster.com.
Manufactured in the United States of America 0322 LAK
2 4 6 8 10 9 7 5 3
Library of Congress Control Number 2019950433
ISBN 978-1-5344-4140-8 (hc)
ISBN 978-1-5344-4139-2 (pbk)
ISBN 978-1-5344-4141-5 (eBook)

Bug Dipping, Bug Sipping

by Marilyn Singer

illustrated by Lucy Semple

Ready-to-Read

Simon Spotlight

New York   London   Toronto   Sydney   New Delhi

Bug on the water,
dipping.

Bug on the flower, sipping.

Bug on the roses,
zinging.

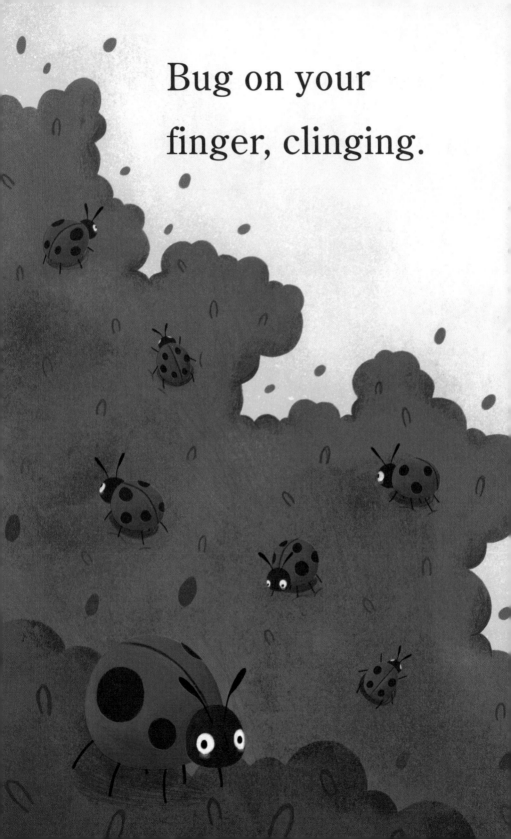

Bug on your
finger, clinging.

Bug in the tall grass,
leaping.

Bug on the lampshade, sleeping.

Bug on the ceiling,
crawling.

Bug in the meadow,
calling.

Bug in the treetop,
flashing.

Bug on the sidewalk,
dashing.

Bug underground,
rising.

Bug on a branch,
disguising.

Bug by the back door,
spinning.

Bug at the front door, grinning.

What kind of bug is that?

BUG FACTS

- Big dragonflies swoop over lakes, ponds, marshes, and other bodies of water to catch bugs to eat. They dip in water to lay eggs that turn into other dragonflies.

- Butterflies get their food from flowers. Their wings are often brightly colored and patterned. They fly in the daytime.

- Bees drink from flowers and gather yellow pollen to feed their young. They won't sting if you leave them alone.

- The most familiar ladybugs are red with black spots. Their color warns birds not to eat them because they taste bad.

- Grasshoppers can fly, but they also jump high with their strong hind legs. Some types flash bright colors when they leap to startle enemies.

- Moths and butterflies are cousins. Most moths are not as colorful as butterflies, and they usually fly at night.

- Flies zip and zoom with ease. They can also stick to the walls and hang upside down.

- Crickets are easier to hear than to see. In the evening, male crickets chirp by rubbing their wings together to find females, and to chase away other males.

- Fireflies come out at night. Male fireflies call to females with a pattern of glowing or flashing lights. Females answer back with their own pattern.

- Most ants cannot fly. They can walk fast and carry heavy loads.

- Depending on the type, young cicadas stay underground, eating roots, for one to seventeen years. Then they dig their way out and shed their outer covering. These adult cicadas sing in the trees to find mates.

- Stick insects look like twigs to fool enemies who want to eat them. Also called walking sticks, they eat leaves and do not bite. They are among the longest insects in the world!

- We call it a bug, but it's not an insect—it's a spider. Insects have six legs. Spiders have eight. The spider in this book spins webs to catch the insects it eats.

We call small crawly or flying creatures "bugs." They live on land and in the water everywhere on Earth. Most of the bugs in this book are insects. There are more than a million kinds of insects—more than any other animal. An insect has six legs and a hard outer covering. Its body is divided into three main parts. Many insects have wings and feelers. They eat many different kinds of foods—plants, nectar, other insects, blood, or even your lunch! Some insects have mouths that chew food, and some have mouths that suck it up. Some can bite or sting, but most don't. Still, unless you know for sure a bug won't hurt you, it's better to look and not touch. But since they are such fascinating creatures, please do look!

Bugs are everywhere, indoors and outside. How many can you find?